D1151313

# Olive Leaf Extract
## Potent Antibacterial, Antiviral and Antifungal Agent

by
## Jack Ritchason, N.D.

---

**Ask in-store for**
## Comvita Olive Leaf Complex

Extracted directly from
*fresh-picked* olive leaves to ensure
the maximum presence of natural,
healthy compounds.

www.comvita.co.uk

---

© 2000

Published in Australia by:
Bizmoore Pty Ltd
bizmoore@bigpond.com

The information in this book is for educational purposes only and is not recommended as a means of diagnosing or treating an illness. All matters concerning physical and mental health should be supervised by a health practitioner knowledgeable in treating that particular condition. Neither the publisher nor author directly or indirectly dispense medical advice, nor do they prescribe any remedies or assume any responsibility for those who choose to treat themselves.

# Contents

# Olive Leaf Extract:
# An Introduction

It is no secret that the general public is constantly searching for ways to improve their health and ultimately the quality of their lives. More and more, we are bombarded with information (some accurate, some not) concerning weight loss, avoiding baldness, enhancing energy, reversing cancer, relieving arthritis, eliminating migraines, and a myriad of other health issues. Of recent concern has been the idea that current antibiotic drugs, once hailed as conventional medicine's most powerful weapons, now face being relegated to the status of obsolete. Why? With the widespread use of these antibiotics, the targeted microbes have slowly but surely developed ways to render the drugs useless. More and more health experts predict that even the most common bacterial infections may one day pose serious health problems.

In response to this apparent threat, a natural, safe, and effective "phytomedicinal" has emerged as a powerful weapon in the fight against microbial infections. What is this weapon? The olive leaf, whose extract has been used for centuries in many cultures for medicinal purposes, and which has been studied extensively by the modern scientific world. And not only is olive leaf extract effective against pathological microbes—bacteria, viruses, fungi, and parasites—but it apparently has a variety of other health benefits as well. The following is a summarized list of this potent herbal's apparent health benefits:

- Effective inhibition and prevention of infection by wide range of pathological microbes, including viruses, bacteria, retroviruses, fungi, parasites, yeasts, and moulds.

- The enhancement of elasticity of arteries, which improves blood flow, reduces high blood pressure, and prevents the progression of other forms of heart disease.

- The relief of inflammation related to arthritis, especially rheumatoid arthritis.

- Improvement in symptoms of chronic fatigue syndrome and related disorders.

- Ability to fight free radical production.

- Prevention and treatment of many types of viral infections, including the herpes viruses, most influenza and common cold viruses, Epstein-Barr viruses, the HIV virus, the cytomegalovirus, and others.

- Eradication of candidiasis and associated yeast syndromes.

- Effective eradication of a variety of parasites, from microscopic protozoa to intestinal worms.

- Enhancement of energy production in the body.

- Relief from toothaches, painful haemorrhoids, athlete's foot, mycotic nails, and various other annoying conditions.

# Historical Use of Olive Leaf Extract

The earliest known use of olive leaf for medicinal purposes appears to come from the ancient Egyptians. In their culture, the olive leaf was regarded as a symbol of heavenly power. Consequently, they used the extracted oils of the leaf as a part of the mummification rituals of their kings.

Of course, numerous other cultures have used the olive leaf (and tree and fruit) for nutritional and medicinal purposes. Especially in Mediterranean cultures, the olive leaf was used for a variety of health conditions, including infections, fever, and pain.

Late in the 19th century, scientists investigating olive leaf's medicinal properties isolated a phenolic compound, to which they assigned the name "oleuropein." Most researchers considered this the component most responsible for olive leaf's therapeutic abilities. In 1962, an Italian researcher reported that oleuropein lowered blood pressure in animals. This set off a rush of investigative research targeted towards the olive leaf and its potential as a medicinal agent.

The results of research coming out at this time were promising. European teams confirmed the finding that oleuropein could lower blood pressure. Additionally, results indicated that it could also positively affect blood flow, prevent intestinal muscle spasms, and relieve arrhythmia.

Then, a research team from the Netherlands was able to isolate the active ingredient in oleuropein, a substance later called elenolic acid.

These and other studies led Upjohn, a major American pharmaceutical company, to investigate elenolic acid's ability to fight viruses. By the late 1960s, Upjohn was able to show that elenolic acid could indeed inhibit the growth of viruses. In fact, the elenolic acid was so powerful that it stopped every virus that it was tested against. Of most importance was elenolic acid's apparent ability to counteract a variety of viruses known to cause the common cold in humans.

In addition to this research, interest was being generated in another form of elenolic acid, calcium elenolate, and its therapeutic capabilities. Lab experiments consequently showed that calcium elenolate was able to fight viruses, bacteria, and parasitic agents. In fact, the compound worked so well that the researchers eventually determined that the compound was not only effective, but also completely safe and nontoxic, even at high doses.

These results led to further research, including animal tests. Here, scientists encountered something unexpected. While the substance was well tolerated, it also rapidly attached itself to blood proteins upon being introduced into the body. This process of attachment, the researchers eventually decided, basically rendered it useless. Despite further research, any attempt to develop and approve a pharmaceutical virus and bacteria killing drug was stopped.

Consequently, no patented antiviral drug was developed (and to this writing, there are no patented antiviral drugs). Nevertheless, interest in the olive leaf and its potent compounds has continued, mainly in Europe. To date, there have been some very promising findings. These include the following:

- Pharmacologists at the University of Granada discovered that extract from the olive leaf can promote relaxation of the arterial walls. In addition to preventing heart disease, this finding also suggests that olive leaf extract may be pivotal in fighting hypertension (high blood pressure). Other research supports the notion that olive leaf extract reduces high blood pressure, as well as stabilizes blood sugar levels, which has possible ramifications for diabetes sufferers.

- One research team has determined that oleuropein may be able to inactivate bacteria by dissolving the outer lining of individual cells.

- Researcher's at the University of Milan found that oleuropein inhibited oxidation of low-density lipoproteins, the "bad cholesterol" involved in the formation of various types of heart disease. This finding appears to be confirmed by further research, which indicates that oleuropein may contain valuable antioxidant properties.

These and other findings offer the world exciting possibilities in the health care world. Researchers in America are now taking another serious look at olive leaf extract, and products are currently lining the shelves of health food stores. It appears that this new herbal has a promising future.

# Clinical Perspectives Concerning Olive Leaf Extract

Health professionals in this country began using olive leaf extract early in 1995 when it first became commercially available. Although long-term perspectives as to olive leaf's capabilities are still somewhat unclear, initial results are very positive. This plant certainly appears to be a unique and exciting mix that offers an array of therapeutic benefits for various common health conditions.

While folk use and medical research indicates that olive leaf extract is a promising medicinal agent, it must be remembered that it cannot be considered a "miracle" or cure-all supplement. To be most effective, olive leaf extract, like most nutritional supplements, should be part of a holistic health plan that involves nutritional and dietary considerations, sufficient exercise, safe lifestyle habits, stress reduction, and other healthy practices. In addition, it is necessary to remember that not all people are the same. While some may experience incredible benefits with a supplement like olive leaf extract, others may see only moderate results. Each individual must learn to tailor his or her own health and dietary habits according to their specific situations and needs. Of course, it is probably safe to say that olive leaf extract can play a very beneficial role in the path to achieving great health.

# Principal Health Benefits of Olive Leaf Extract

As you can see in the previous list of health benefits attributed to olive leaf extract, it is apparent that this powerful herbal can have a profound effect on infection by viral, bacterial or other microbial agents. This has far-reaching effects. For instance, the common cold may cease to be such a dreaded occurrence with the use of olive leaf. The flu's devastating effects may be overcome with the use of olive leaf extract. Simple infections could be easily treatable with the herbal. And more serious types of infections that previously were dangerous and costly, may have found their match in the wonderfully adept antiviral and antibacterial agent, olive leaf extract.

# Antibacterial/Antiviral Properties of Olive Leaf Extract

To really show how effective olive leaf extract and its various constituents are against viruses and bacteria, the following provides a comprehensive listing of the viruses, bacteria and other fungi/parasites against which it has been shown to be effective. This list comes principally from the researchers at Upjohn, the company that first stirred widespread interest in researching olive leaf extract. These researchers found olive leaf extract to be effective in treating infection by the following viruses: herpes, vaccinia, pseudorabies, Newcastle, Coxsacloe A 21, encepthlomyocarditis, polio 1, 2, and 3, vesicular stomititus, sindbis, retrovirus, Moloney Murine leukemia, Rauscher Murine leukemia, Moloney sarcoma, and many influenza and para-influenza types.

The following are bacteria and parasitic protozoans against which olive leaf extract was shown to be effective in treating: lactobacillus plantarum W50, brevis 50, pediococcus cerevisiae 39, leuconostoc mesenteroides 42, staphylococcus aureus, bacillus subtilis, enterobacteraerogenes NRRL B-199, E. cloacae NRRL B-414, E. coli, Salamonella tyhimurium, pseudomonas fluorescens, P. solanacearum, P. lachrymans, erwinia carotovora, E. tracheiphila, xanthomonas vesicatoria, corynesbacterium Michiganese, plasmodium falciparum, virax and malariae (Privitera, 1996).

# How is Olive Leaf Effective Against Viruses and Bacteria?

Though there are still some questions concerning exactly how olive leaf works in some specific processes, there is still ample data that gives a fairly accurate picture of how the plant provides various therapeutic benefits. Dr. James R. Privitera, M.D., explains these processes.

- Olive leaf extract provides interference with viral infection and/or spreading by "inactivating" specific virus cells or by inhibiting their shedding, budding, and assembly at the cell membrane.

- Olive leaf extract also interferes with certain amino acid production essential for the survival of specific microbes, be it virus, bacterium, parasite, or fungus.

- It also neutralizes the reverse transcriptase and protease production of the retrovirus, which is necessary for the virus to be able to alter the RNA of a healthy human cell.

- Compounds of olive leaf extract can directly penetrate infected human cells and inhibit further microbial reproduction.

- Olive leaf extract also may stimulate directly the formation of immune system cells that combat various types of microbes.

Before going more in depth about the research concerning olive leaf and viruses and bacteria, it would probably be helpful to understand a little more about the nature of bacteria and viruses.

## A LITTLE ABOUT BACTERIA AND VIRUSES

Bacteria are extremely small organisms that can literally be found in nearly every nook and cranny on this planet. They live on and in other live animals (like ourselves) and plants, and can often survive harsh conditions. Bacteria are generally regarded as "bad" by most people, though this is not entirely true. There are numerous types of bacteria that serve useful roles for the environment and for humans; for instance, the bacterium Acidophilus is extremely valuable in aiding digestion and the body's immune function.

However, bacteria can become a nuisance or even dangerous when allowed to grow out of control. Bacteria bring about a diseased condition in various ways. For bacteria to cause an infection, they must enter the body and find a place to multiply in large numbers before the body's defense mechanisms can destroy and remove them. If the bacteria multiply at a rate and quantity that supersedes the body's immune capabilities, the results can be extremely dangerous. As their numbers rise into the billions, these bacteria damage the body by damaging its tissues (often without prejudice) and producing a variety of microtoxins that inflict even more damage.

Bacteria are amazingly adept at changing to fit their environment and circumstances. As mentioned previously, they can replicate at blinding speed inside the host organism, sometimes doubling their population within five minutes. This rapid reproduction can produce genetic mutations that form defenses against the various antibiotic drugs– penicillin or amoxycillin, for example– and effectively render the drugs powerless. In addition, these microbes can then pass on this genetic protection to their offspring.

Until recently, scientists thought they had effectively controlled bacterial infection through the development of antibiotic drugs, of which penicillin was the first. These antibiotics destroyed the growing bacterial colony by one of three means:

1. A large number of antibiotics interfere with the microbe's ability to build its own wall;

2. Other antibiotics, like tetracycline and erythromycin can clog the mechanisms that the bacterial cells use to produce proteins essential to their survival;

3. Other antibiotics adhere or "stick" to the individual bacterial chromosome, essentially prohibiting its reproduction.

To accomplish any of these three, the drug had to either enter the bacterial cell or fit itself onto the receptor site on the outside wall of the bacteria. For years, scientists have been able to develop new and more powerful antibiotics that could achieve these results. However, over the last decade, the scientific and medical worlds are recognizing that even the most powerful antibiotic drug is less and less effective against many of the bacteria it used to easily destroy. As a result, doctors and scientists alike are warning against the development of "superbugs," microbes that have effectively been able to mutate and change to the point that antibiotics are powerless. Genetic mutation is not the only defense these superbugs have developed. Dr. Stuart Levy, M.D., of Tufts University, says that different types of bacteria can "lend" DNA that one may not have to another to allow for reproduction; in addition, research indicates that there are "jumping genes," DNA that can effectively pass from one microbe to another.

The pharmaceutical industry has developed numerous antibiotics to fight bacterial infections, and is supposedly working on the development of dozens more. Despite this, there is the ever-growing fear that no matter what drugs we come up with, our microbial friends will always be one step ahead.

So, what to do? These are reasons enough that we need a new, safe, and natural agent that has proven itself as an effective tool in counteracting the never-ending onslaught of pathological organisms. This brings us to the central topic of this publication— olive leaf extract, which has been proven to provide excellent protection against all microbes detrimental to human health—viruses, bacteria, fungi, and parasites.

# Research Targeting Olive Leaf and Viral/ Bacterial Infection

As discussed in other areas of this booklet, it is now widely known that olive leaf extract is a very effective antiviral and antibacterial agent. Not only do the plant's specific components fight and "kill" these invading pathogens, but it also stimulates the body's own immune system to function more effectively in fighting the microbes. This has far-reaching ramifications for some very common health conditions caused or worsened by infection: the common cold, flu, ear infections, sinus infection, cold sores, some forms of diarrhea, pneumonia, meningitis, strep throat, food poisoning, and a host of others. There is plenty of research to support olive leaf's apparent antiviral/antibacterial properties. The researchers of one study targeting oleuropein's ability to fight specific microbes say:

> *The antimicrobial potential of eight phenolic compounds isolated from olive cake was tested against the growth of Escherichia coli, Klebsiella pneumoniae, Bacillus cereus, Aspergillus flavus and Aspergillus parasiticus. . . .*

> *Oleuropein, and p-hydroxy benzoic, vanillic and p-coumaric*
> *acids (0.4 mg/ml) completely inhibited the growth of E. coli,*
> *K. pneumoniae and B. cereus. (Aziz, et al., 43)*

As we all know, E. coli (Escherichia coli) poisoning is involved in causing all sorts of gastrointestinal discomfort, including cramping and severe diarrhea. Bacillus cereus will not only cause severe diarrhea, but can also lead to other serious conditions, even death; additionally, K. pneumoniae is a culprit in respiratory tract infections.

Other studies have specifically targeted olive leaf extract's ability to fight the common cold, flu, and other related conditions, and have demonstrated amazing results. One such study, conducted by researchers at the R Clinic in Budapest, Hungary, found that treatment with olive leaf extract helped over 90 percent of 164 patients with respiratory and lung conditions.

# Fungal, Yeast and Parasitic Infections

While it is true that the average life span of humans has drastically increased, the level of overall health has not enjoyed such an increase. Numerous studies show that a significant cause of many of today's most common health concerns involve infection by parasites, fungi and yeasts. These organisms can infect nearly every area of the body, and if left untreated, can be extremely difficult to eradicate. Parasites can range from microscopic amoebas to 25-foot tapeworms. Fungus can infect the skin, finger and toenails, and yeast can easily hold back an already weakened immune system.

There are many factors involved in the onset of such infection: diet, use of antibiotic and other drugs, lifestyle practices, lack of exercise, etc. There are also many things to consider when determining the best route to overcome infection by the offending agent. However, olive leaf extract offers a promising alternative in the treatment protocol. It has been shown to be effective against Candida albicans, Candida krusei, oral candidiasis, vaginitis yeast syndrome, cryptosporidia, giardia, pinworms, tapeworms, ringworm, malaria-causing protozoa, and many others.

Besides the clinical research that demonstrates olive leaf extract is effective against fungal and yeast infections, there is a wealth of data from personal case histories of individuals using it for similar purposes. Common uses include chronic toenail fungus infection ,which inflicts literally millions of Americans, and which is widely ignored, This condition affects a wide range of people: athletes; sufferers of diabetes, cancer, and AIDS; the elderly; those who stand a lot or wear the same shoes all the time; and those who use artificial nails. Obviously, drugs taken for cancer, AIDS, and other conditions lower the body's resistance and make it easier for this type of infection to occur.

The conventional medical world has developed a new medication for this type of infection. However, it is very expensive compared to olive leaf extract (it costs approximately $300 for a month's supply). There are too many personal experiences of patients successfully using olive leaf extract to overcome fungal infection to ignore its apparent benefits. Patients with candidiasis have attested to olive leaf extracts ability to improve their condition. Consumption of the supplement has led to fewer allergic reactions, enhanced energy levels, fewer infections, and an overall feeling of great health.

# Coronary Dilating Action of Olive Leaf Extract

Since 1977, when trials began in Bulgaria, olive leaf extract (and specifically its constituent oleuropein) has been the source of great interest concerning coronary dilation (the expanding/contracting ability of the arteries). Compared against other plant substances, oleuropein displayed a clear ability to promote healthy dilatatory action in coronary arteries. In fact, the results of these studies were extremely impressive. When oleuropein was administered, the coronary artery blood flow in the laboratory animals increased by more than 50 percent, indeed a significant increase.

In addition to the coronary artery dilating effect, oleuropein displayed other cardiovascular health-enhancing effects. These same studies showed that it was active against barium chloride-induced arrhythmia and against calcium-induced arrhythmia, as well as inducing a long-lasting effect of lowering elevated blood pressure. Of course, these studies, like all others, indicated that olive leaf extract and its individual constituents were extremely safe and non-toxic.

# Olive Leaf Extract and Hypertension

Another area of extreme interest concerning olive leaf extract has been that of lowering high blood pressure. As stated earlier, the University of Granada conducted experiments showing that oleuropeoside, another component present in the extract of the olive leaf, may be responsible for the vasodilator effect on the smooth muscle layer of coronary arteries. Say the researchers:

> *We studied the importance of the smooth vascular muscle endothelium in the vasodilator action of the decoction of olive (Olea europaea) leaf. We also showed that oleuropeoside is a component responsible for vasodilator activity but, from the results, it seems likely that at least one other principle is to be found in the olive leaf which is either a vasodilator itself or else potentiates the relaxant effect of oleuropeoside. (Zarzuelo, et al., 417)*

In other words, it appears that oleuropeoside can reduce high blood pressure levels by causing constricted arteries to relax and become more flexible, thereby allowing for more blood flow. They also note that there is probably at least one other component that aids oleuropeoside in this relaxation process.

Earlier studies confirm the findings of the University of Granada. In Bulgaria, it was first hypothesized that oleuropein also can have a beneficial effect on elevated blood pressure. In fact, studies at the Department of Experimental and Clinical Pharmacology of the Postgraduate Medical Institute showed that it could reduce high blood pressure levels by an average of 68 percent of the initial level in some animals, and as high as 36 percent in other animals. The Bulgarian team also found that coronary blood flow was significantly increased, and irregular heart beat (arrhythmia) was corrected upon administration of olive leaf extract.

So, if olive leaf extract appears to be a powerful agent that enhances cardiovascular health, why have so few people heard of it? While that question remains a bit unclear, it is certain that the original researchers who targeted olive leaf extract remain optimistic that today's consumer will soon recognize its value. Dr. Morton Walker, respected medical journalist says, "That's a shame, because almost twenty years have been lost in which millions of people throughout the world could have had their elevated blood pressures lowered to normal, their atherosclerotic arteries unhardened, and their heart arteries dilated without resorting to life-threatening coronary bypass surgery" (Walker, 78).

# Olive Leaf Extract's Antioxidant Effects

Most scientists and researchers familiar with olive leaf extract recognize oleuropein as its major component responsible for a variety of health benefits in humans. One of these benefits is that of combating free radical damage to individual cells. Say researchers from the University of Milan:

> *Plants in the Mediterranean basin, such as vine and olive trees, have developed an array of antioxidant defenses to protect themselves from environmental stress. Accordingly, the incidence of coronary heart disease and certain cancers is lower in the Mediterranean area, where olive oil is the dietary fat of choice. As opposed to other vegetable oils, extra virgin olive oil, which is obtained by physical pressure from a whole fruit, is rich in phenolic components that are responsible for the particular stability of the oil. We have investigated the scavenging actions of some olive oil phenolics, namely hydroxytyrosol and oleuropein, with respect to superoxide anion generation, neutrophils respiratory burst, and hypochlorous acid. [The results] indicate that both compounds are potent scavengers of*

*superoxide radicals: whenever demonstrated in vivo, these properties may partially explain the observed lower incidence of CHD and cancer associated with the Mediterranean diet (Visioli, et al., 60).*

Another study by Visioli and team targeted oleuropein's ability to act as a free radical scavenger. Again, this study was also successful in demonstrating oleuropein's antioxidant effect. Says the published report on the study:

*The Mediterranean diet, rich in fruit, vegetables, grain, and vegetable oil (mainly olive oil) is correlated with a lower incidence of coronary heart disease (CHD). Natural antioxidants contained in the Mediterranean diet might also play a role in the prevention of cardiovascular diseases, through inhibition of LDL oxidation. Oleuropein 10(-5) M effectively inhibited CuSO4-induced LDL oxidation, as assessed by various parameters. We demonstrate in this investigation that polyphenolic components of the Mediterranean diet interfere with biochemical events that are implicated in atherogenetic disease [types of cardiovascular disease], thus proposing a new link between the Mediterranean diet and prevention of CHD (Visioli, Galli, 1965).*

# Olive Leaf Extract and Hypoglycemia/ Diabetes

As mentioned earlier, researchers at the University of Granada in Spain found that extract from the olive leaf could have a significant effect on the management of blood sugar levels. The authors of the study stated, "The hypoglycemic activity of olive leaf was studied. One of the compounds responsible for this activity was oleuropeoside, which showed activity at a dose of 16 mg/kg. This compound also demonstrated antidiabetic activity in animals with alloxan-induced diabetes. The hypoglycemic activity of this compound may result from two mechanisms: (a) potentiation of glucose-induced insulin release, and (b) increased peripheral uptake of glucose" (Gonzalez, et al., 513). In other words, the researchers hypothesize that oleuropein could actually stimulate the production of insulin (which plays a key role in the utilization of blood sugar) or in the enhancement of utilization of blood sugar in the extremities (outer areas of the body).

# Increased Energy Levels with Use of Olive Leaf Extract

One of the most frequent comments heard from patients after taking olive leaf extract is that they experience a dramatic increase in energy levels and have a greater sense of well-being (In fact, some patients experience such a dramatic increase in energy that they inquire whether there is an "upper" ingredient in the product). Also very intriguing to many health experts is the fact that many patients want to continue taking olive leaf even after their treatment program has taken care of specific problems.

Improvement in energy levels can also be seen specifically in "fatigue" type disorders, such as chronic fatigue syndrome, lupus, mononucleosis, Epstein-Barr, fibromyalgia, etc. Most doctors would consider abnormal fatigue levels to be the number one complaint heard from patients. Of course, if these people would improve their dietary and exercise habits, they would all experience some improvement in energy levels and reducing fatigue. However, olive leaf represents an "easy" way to quickly fight the problem.

# Other Conditions Treatable with Olive Leaf Extract

Of course, there are numerous other symptoms and conditions that are a result of viral, bacterial and fungal infection. Herpes, AIDS, fibromyalgia, chronic fatigue, arthritis, and other auto-immune disorders all have direct connections to problems associated with the immune system and its inability to function correctly. Olive leaf extract can only help a debilitated immune system begin the process of recuperating to the point of effectively fighting any type of infection that may be present.

For instance, in 1969 Dr. Renis of the Upjohn company found that a compound of oleuropein from the olive leaf could kill all viruses, including the herpes virus, against which it was tested. The virucidal activity of oleuropein was due to its interaction with the protein coat of the virus and not with its genetic material. In 1992, French biologists working at the Laboratoire de Pharmacognosie discovered that all of the herpes viruses were inhibited in their activity or killed by olive leaf extract. Even more impressive was the support they provided to their findings by citing 28 references to the virucidal qualities of oleuropein.

In addition to herpes, the use of olive leaf extract has become very popular for symptoms associated with chronic fatigue syndrome (CFS) and related disorders. Though not completely understood, CFS is known to be associated with immune dysfunction, which allows infections with a variety of opportunistic microbes (herpes-viruses, retroviruses, fungi, parasites, etc.). Many sufferers of chronic fatigue syndrome may suffer from candidiasis (an overgrowth of the yeast Candida albicans), or have a chronic active infection of the Epstein-Barr Virus. Recent research indicates that by the end of early adulthood, nearly all Americans have detectable levels of EBV anti-bodies in their blood, meaning that they have at some stage been infected by this virus. Of course, in those with a healthy immune system the virus stays dormant and does not produce any symptoms.

There is some very interesting research concerning chronic fatigue syndrome that may be of interest to users of olive leaf extract. Dr. W.J. Martin, head of molecular immunopathology at the University of Southern California Medical Center, has discovered some strange retroviruses commonly known as "foamy viruses" in a high percentage of patients with CFS. These people commonly complain of persistent debilitating, flu-like symptoms similar to those associated with CFS. Other viruses that are being studied as possible causes of CFS are HTLV-2, entero-viruses such as the polio virus, herpes-virus type VI and the cytomegalovirus. These kinds of viruses are detectable in most people but are usually in a dormant state. Until the virus fighting properties of olive leaf extract were recently rediscovered and proved, there has been very little specific treatment to overcome virally induced CFS. But according to recent findings and hundreds of users of olive leaf extract, it now appears possible to effectively fight these viruses by taking sufficient quantities of olive leaf extract capsules in repeated doses.

# Immune Function: Key to Great Health

Many people often wonder how their immune system is performing. Is it functioning well, or are there areas that need improvement? The following are questions you can ask yourself to determine if indeed you may be suffering from immune dysfunction (and therefore a good candidate for using olive leaf extract).

- Do you have recurrent viral infections?
- Do you have herpes (genital and/or cold sores)?
- Do you suffer from frequent colds and flu?
- Do you experience inflammation and/or infection in the upper respiratory tract e.g.. sinuses, ear infections, sore throats, or swollen cervical gland, on a fairly regular basis?
- Do you suffer from recurrent bronchitis?
- Have you had recurrent cystitis?
- Do you suffer from recurrent skin infections
- Have you been diagnosed with chronic fatigue syndrome?
- Have you suffered from recurrent infections of Candida or other yeast?
- Have you been diagnosed with Epstein-Barr?
- Do you experience reduced stamina and resistance when under stress?

• Are your levels of energy constantly below normal?

## TIPS ON IMPROVING IMMUNE FUNCTION

The following are some good tips to boosting immune function, and ultimately achieving improved levels of health.

• Eat immune boosting foods such as raw fruits and vegetables, raw garlic and onion, raw vegetable juices, raw fenugreek, chilli, ginger, free range eggs, oily fish (salmon, sardines, tuna), avocados, fresh wheat-germ, flaxseed (ground freshly and cold pressed oil), barley grass ( juice or sprouted seeds), wheat-grass juice, freshly sprouted seeds and beans, cold pressed seed and vegetable oils, fresh seafood, legumes, raw nuts and seeds.

• Sea-weeds such as kelp, dulse, agar-agar, nori, arame, kombu, wakame and hijiki are excellent for improved immune function.

• Cruciferous vegetables like broccoli, cauliflower, cabbage, brussel sprouts and kohlrabi contain phyto-nutrients that protect against infections and cancer. Foods containing plant hormones (known as phyto-estrogens), such as isoflavones and lignans, are known to reduce the risk of many cancers. Good sources of these plant hormones are soy beans and their products, alfalfa and flaxseed.

• Ensure adequate intake of the most important minerals for the immune system—magnesium 400 mg daily, zinc chelate 20 mg daily, and selenium 200 mcg daily. These minerals are needed for immune function and are anti-inflammatory.

• Avoid mucous producing foods— animal milks, cheese, ice-cream, cream, preserved meats, and processed foods are the biggest culprits.

• Avoid tobacco, smoking and alcohol.

• Drink 8 to 10 glasses of filtered water daily.

• Make regular exercise a part of your daily regimen. Exercise can do wonders for a poorly functioning immune system and promote health in various other ways.

- Ensure adequate vitamin C intake by eating citrus fruits, red and green peppers, kiwi, tomatoes, and take a supplement of approximately 1000–2000 mg.

- Finally, take olive leaf extract. A good dose to maintain is one 500-mg capsule twice daily. It is recommended that you take brands that contain at least 10 percent of the active ingredient, oleuropein. Regarding liquid olive leaf extract, a good maintenance dose is one 5ml teaspoonful, twice a day.

# Summary of Conditions for Which Olive Leaf Extract Acts as a Microbial Agent

| | |
|---|---|
| AIDS | amoebiasis |
| anthrax | athlete's foot |
| bladder infection | campylobacter |
| chicken pox | chlamydia |
| cholera | common cold |
| cold sore (herpes simplex I) | cryptosporidiosis |
| cytomegalovirus | diarrheal disease |
| diptheria | ear infection |
| Ebola Sudan virus | E. coli |
| Epstein-Barr virus | flu (influenza) |
| gastric ulcers (from H. pylori) | genital herpes/warts |
| giardia | gonorrhea |
| group B strep | hantavirus |
| hepatitis A, B, C | herpes zoster (shingles) |
| lyme disease | malaria |
| measles | meningitis (bacterial) |
| meningitis (viral) | mononucleosis |
| pinworms | pneumonia, bacterial |
| pneumonia, viral | polio |

pork tapeworm
rheumatic fever
retrovirus infection
rotavirus infection
salmonella
staphyloccocal food poisoning
syphillis
thrush
trichinosis
urinary tract infections
warts

rabies
ringworm
roundworm
RSV
smallpox
strep throat
tuberculosis
toxic shock syndrome
typhoid fever
vaginal yeast infections

# The Herxheimer or "Die-Off" Effect

When people ask if there are any side effects to using olive leaf extract, the answer is generally a resounding "no." However, when olive leaf extract is being used to treat a chronic condition, there may sometimes occur an adverse, albeit healthy, reaction. This is what is generally referred to as the "Herxheimer" or "die-off" effect. So what exactly is the "die-off" effect? While living in the body, most of the offending microbes somehow manage to evade the body's immune system. However, upon exposure to olive leaf extract, large numbers of the pathological microbes will die. Soon after, their cell-wall proteins (which are essentially toxins) are absorbed through the weakened mucous membrane. The body then begins its natural processes to get rid of these toxins; however, if present in numbers too large for the eliminative system to handle, the individual may develop symptoms that include headaches, swelling in the mouth, throat, sinuses, and lymphatics, rashes, fatigue, diarrhea, muscle/joint achiness, or other flu-like symptoms. Obviously, severity will vary from person to person, depending on the extent of their condition, the state of their immune and eliminatory systems, and how much olive leaf extract is being consumed.

To any average reader, the previous list may make it hard to want to start taking olive leaf extract. However, one must keep in mind that despite the obvious unpleasantness associated with these symptoms, they are very desirable because they indicate that the body is effectively eliminating the infecting organisms. In other words, the presence of "die-off" effect suggests that the patient is having an excellent response to the olive leaf treatment. Needless to say, anyone who experiences the "die-off" effect generally feels fabulously well afterwards, many times better than ever before.

Some of you may ask if there is anything to do to minimize the effects of the die-off effect. Yes, there is. Many physicians recommend that an individual consume plenty of water in between usages of the product. Plenty of water helps keep the lymphatic system and the kidneys functioning properly and more capable of handling excess toxins. If the symptoms of die-off are too uncomfortable for an individual, it may be a good idea to either reduce the dose of olive leaf extract, or go off it completely for a day or two before slowly increasing the dose once again. It can take anywhere from a couple days to a week to completely rid the body of the excess toxins.

# Dosage, Availability and Safety of Olive Leaf Extract Products

Until recently, only a few health professionals in the United States and Canada (and most of them in the "alternative" health care arena) have had any knowledge of the exciting therapeutic possibilities of olive leaf extract. However, as mentioned earlier, the procedures necessary for an acceptable product were approved in 1995, and sales to this country began in 1996. (This was mainly due to the lack of information available to the public and health communities.) But as more and more of the research targeting olive leaf extract comes to light, this herbal is fast becoming one of the most exciting and promising products distributed worldwide.

Though there is no "official" dosage for taking olive leaf extract, some experts recommend a maintenance dose for general use and a "therapeutic" dose for specific disorders. The most popular amount for the maintenance dose is one 500-mg capsule, twice daily (preferably just before eating). For conditions such as the common cold, flu, sinus infections, and basic respiratory tract infections, the recommended dose is two 500-mg capsules every six hours. For acute infections such as sore throat, swollen glands, fever, etc., the recommendation is three 500-mg capsules every six hours. If a high-strength liquid olive leaf extract is being used, one 5ml teaspoonful is approximately equivalent to one 500mg capsule.

The liquid olive leaf extracts have the benefit of being able to be taken internally as well as being applied externally to the skin when being used for skin conditions. The liquids are also more effective for mouth and throat conditions as they directly touch the affected areas. Liquids are also more quickly and easily absorbed by the body when taken orally.

Concerning side effects of using olive leaf extract, the most common (though not truly a side effect) is that of the die-off effect that results in headache, fatigue, pain, etc. If this happens, reduce dose by half or discontinue the capsules for 3 days, then start again on reduced dosages.

From all indications (research, case studies, and widespread use), olive leaf extract appears to be an extremely safe supplement that can effectively aid the body in improving immune function and fighting infection by various microbes.

# References

Aziz NH, Farag SE, Mousa LA, Abo-Zaid MA. "Comparative antibacterial and antifungal effects of some phenolic compounds." Microbios 1998;93(384):43-54.

Cruess WV, and Alsberg CL, The bitter glucoside of the olive. J. Amer. Chem. Soc. 1934; 56:2115-7.

Department of Pharmacology and Toxicology, Society of Pharmaceutical Industries of Tunis, Hypotension, hypoglycemia and hypouricemia recorded after repeated administration of aqueous leaf extract of Olea europaea, Belgian Pharmacology Journal, March-April 1994; 49(2), 101-8.

Duarte, J., et al. "Effects of oleuropeoside in isolated guinea-pig atria." Planta Med 1993 Aug;59(4):318-22. Department of Pharmacology, School of Pharmacy, University of Granada, Spain.

Elliott GA et al, Preliminary studies with calcium elenolate, an antiviral agent. Antimicrob. Agents Chemother., 1970; 173-76.

Gariboldi P et al, Secoiridoids from olea europaea, Phytochem., 1986; 25(4)865-69.

Gonzales, M., et al. "Hypoglycemic activity of olive leaf." Planta Med 1992 Dec;58(6):513-5. Departamento de Farmacologia, Facultad de Farmacia, Universidad de Granada, Spain.

Heinze JE et al, Specificity of the antiviral agent calcium elenolate. Antimicrob. Agents

Hirschman SZ, Inactivation of DNA polymerases of Murine Leukaemia viruses by calcium elenolate. Nature New Biology, 1972; 238:277-79.

Juven B et al, Studies on the mechanism of the antimicrobial action of oleuropein. J. Appl. Bact., 1972; 35:559-67.

Kubo I et al, A mutichemical defense mechanism of bitter olive olea europaea (Oleaceae)—Is oleuropein a phytoalexin precursor? J. Chem. Ecol 1985; 11(2):251-63.

Panizzi L et al, The constitution of oleuropein, a bitter glucoside of the olive with hypotensive action. Gazz. Chim. Ital; 1960; 90:1449-85.

Petkov V and Manolov P, Pharmacological analysis of the iridoid oleuropein. Drug Res., 1972; 22(9); 1476-86.

Renis HE, In vitro antiviral activity of calcium elenolate. Antimicrob. Agents Chemother., 1970; 167-72.

Samuelsson G, The blood pressure lowering factor in leaves of Olea Europaea. Farmacevtisk Revy, 1951; 15: 229-39

Soret MG, Antiviral activity of calcium elenolate on parainfluenza infection of hamsters. Antimicrob. Agents Chemother., 1970; 160-66.

Veer WLC et al, A compound isolated from olea europaea. Recueil, 1957; 76:839-40

Visioli F and Galli C, Oleuropein protects low density liproprotein from oxidation, Life Sciences, 1994; 55(24), 1965-71.

Walker, Morton. Olive Leaf Extract. New York; Kensington, 1997.

Zarzuelo A et al, Vasodilator effect of olive leaf, Planta Med., 1991; 57 (5),417-9.

Ziyyat, A., et al. "Phytotherapy of hypertension and diabetes in oriental Morocco." J Ethnopharmacol 1997 Sep; 58(1):45-54. Department of Biology, University Mohamed the First, Faculty of Sciences, Oujda, Morocco.